THE TEN BEST CASINO BETS

By

Henry Tamburin

Research Services Unlimited
P.O. Box 19727
Greensboro, NC 27419

Address all inquiries to the publisher:

> Research Services Unlimited
> P.O. Box 19727
> Greensboro, NC 27419

Second Edition
ISBN: 0-912177-07-1
Library of Congress catalog card number:
93-083953
Seventh Printing, August 2001

PRINTED IN THE UNITED STATES OF AMERICA

The material contained in this book is intended to inform and educate the reader and in no way represents an inducement to gamble legally or illegally.

Preface

A lot has happened in the casinos since the first edition of this book some 18 years ago. For one, the casinos have introduced many new games in addition to blackjack, craps, roulette and baccarat. These new games include: video poker, pai gow poker, sic bo, mini-baccarat, pokette, red dog, multiple action blackjack, pai gow, and others. The mathematical analysis of these new games has resulted in a modification of the ten best casino bets and an updated second edition of this book.

Table of Contents

Preface iii

Introduction 1

Best Bet #1, Blackjack 3

Best Bet #2, Pass Line/Come with Odds ... 19

Best Bet #3, Don't Pass/
    Don't Come with Odds 25

Best Bet #4 & #5, Bank Hand/
    Player Hand 31

Best Bet #6, Place Bets on 6 and 8 37

Best Bet #7, Video Poker 41

Best Bet #8, 4 and 10 Lay Bet 45

Best Bet #9, Pai Gow Poker 49

Best Bet #10, Single O Roulette 59

Betting Strategies 63

Money Management 69

Psychology of Gambling 73

Summary 77

Recommended Reading 79

Index 80

INTRODUCTION

Which bet is your best bet? When you enter a casino, there are over 50 kinds of wagers available to you to choose from. But some offer much better odds than others. These bets are the ones that an intelligent casino player makes to maximize the chances of winning. Or to put it another way, you must only wager on these ten best bets if you ever expect to be a consistent, winning player. It's that simple.

How, you might ask, are these ten best bets determined. Very simply, they are the results of comparing what the casino pays you when you win a bet versus the true mathematical chances of winning that bet. This comparison gives a number which is called the casino's advantage. The higher the casino's advantage, the less likely will be your chances of consistently winning that bet. Thus, you must limit yourself to making only those bets that have the lowest casino advantage.

The casino advantage is often expressed in terms of a percent. Thus, a bet on the joker on the Big Six Wheel has a calculated casino advantage of 15%. What does this mean? It means that the casino stands to win, over the long run, about 15% of the wagers made on this bet.

Keep in mind that the casino advantage is based on the total amount wagered on a particular bet, and not a player's gaming bankroll. Thus, a player who might bring a $50 bankroll to the tables will make many more times this amount in wagers. If he bets $1 on the joker on every spin of the wheel, and assuming 75 spins per hour, then after 1 hour the gambler has made a total of $75 in wagers on the joker. If he plays for 2 hours, his total wagers now add up to $150. After 2 hours of playing in this manner, the 15% casino advantage for this bet tells us that the casino expects to win 15% of the $150.00 wagered or $22.50. This is the casino's expected win based on its mathematical or casino advantage. The casino could win more than $22.50 or perhaps less, but the mathematical probabilities tell us that over the long run, the casino's expected win will approach 15% of all the money wagered on the joker.

You shouldn't begrudge the casinos for their advantage, after all they cannot depend upon luck to generate the income they need to pay their daily expenses. The trick is "to make the other guy pay the casino overhead" by only making bets where the casino advantage is the lowest possible. If you do this and have a little luck at the tables, you have the best chance of being a winner and the least chance of losing your shirt.

So let's now begin to learn what the TEN BEST BETS IN A CASINO are and how to make them.

Best Bet #1
BLACKJACK

The best bet in a casino is playing blackjack with proper playing strategies.[1] The reason is because blackjack is very different mathematically from the other casino games. In most casino games, the odds against winning a bet are fixed and *not* dependent upon what happened on the previous dice throws or roulette spins. With blackjack, this is not the case. Once a freshly shuffled deck or decks of cards are put into play, the odds of winning a particular hand changes and is dependent upon the cards used in previous hands. A player's chances of winning at blackjack always increases if the ratio of cards left in the deck(s) to be played contains an abundance of tens, picture cards and aces. Likewise, if the ratio has an excess of low cards such as 2, 3, 4, 5 and

---

[1]For those new to blackjack, a summary of the basic playing rules can be found on pages 16-18.

6's, then the player's chances of winning are not very good. Thus mathematically we say that blackjack is a game based upon dependent trial processes. In layman's terms, it is a game of skill rather than a game of chance.

It is very easy to program a computer to play blackjack. This is, in fact, how the mathematically correct playing strategies have been determined. Based upon the analysis of millions and millions of computer simulated hands, the playing strategy known as the basic strategy has been developed. IT IS IMPERATIVE TO LEARN THIS BASIC STRATEGY because by using it, you will eliminate the normal 5 to 10% advantage the casino has over the unskilled player. With basic strategy, the casino's advantage, depending upon the rules, is only 0.1 to 0.5%. That is less than a 1% disadvantage for the player, which makes this the best bet in a casino.

The basic strategy is not the same for every game of blackjack dealt in every casino. The strategy depends upon the rules in force. Depending upon the number of decks of cards being used and the rules for pair splitting and doubling down, the basic playing strategy differs slightly. Following is the mathematically correct basic strategy for typical playing rules found in Atlantic City, Nevada, riverboats, dockside casinos, and Indian reservations.

Before you begin to study the basic strategy charts, let us make sure you understand them.

The two variables that determine how you should play your hand are the value of the dealer's upcard and the kind and total of your hand. For example, how should you play the following hand?

Player dealt: Ace, 3. Dealer's upcard is a 2.

Look at Table I and go down the column headed Your Hand to A,3. Now read across. It states: double on 5 or 6 otherwise hit. What this means is that you should double down on your A,3 (soft 14) hand only if the dealer's upcard is a 5 or 6. If it isn't, you should then hit the hand. Since the dealer's upcard is *not* a 5 or 6, you wouldn't double down rather *hit* the hand.

You must learn this basic strategy. Put the strategies for each player hand and dealer upcard on index cards, and go through your cards once or twice a day. When you think you've learned all the strategies, practice playing blackjack at home using the strategies. If you make mistakes in a casino, it could cost you dearly, so practice diligently. If necessary, take a handheld basic strategy card with you to the tables. You can refer to this card if you forget how to make the correct play. You should not, however, use this card as a substitute for memorizing the basic strategy.

Table I
Multiple Deck Basic Strategy
Double-down on any two cards
Double down after pair splitting

Your Hand	Playing Strategy vs. Dealer's Upcard
5 to 8	Always Hit.
9	Double on 3 to 6, otherwise hit.
10	Double on 2 to 9, hit on 10,A.
11	Double on 2 to 10, hit on A.
12	Stand on 4 to 6, otherwise hit.
13	Stand on 2 to 6, otherwise hit.
14	Stand on 2 to 6, otherwise hit.
15	Stand on 2 to 6, otherwise hit.
16	Stand on 2 to 6, otherwise hit.
17	Always stand.
18	Always stand.
A,2	Double on 5, 6, otherwise hit.
A,3	Double on 5, 6, otherwise hit.
A,4	Double on 4 to 6, otherwise hit.
A,5	Double on 4 to 6, otherwise hit.
A,6	Double on 3 to 6, otherwise hit.
A,7	Double on 3 to 6. Stand on 2, 7 or 8. Hit on 9, 10 or A.
A,8 to A,10	Always stand.
A,A	Always split.
2,2	Split on 2 to 7, otherwise hit.
3,3	Split on 2 to 7, otherwise hit.
4,4	Split on 5, 6, otherwise hit.
5,5	Never split. Treat as 10 above.
6,6	Split on 2 to 6, otherwise hit.

7,7	Split on 2 to 7, otherwise hit.
8,8	Always split.
9,9	Split on 2 to 6, 8 or 9.
	Stand on 7, 10, or A.
10,10	Always stand.

This previous multiple deck basic strategy is valid if the players are allowed to double down after pair splitting. If doubling down is *not* allowed after pair splitting, then use the following pair splitting rules.

	Playing Strategy vs.
Your Hand	**Dealer's Upcard**

2,2	Split on 4 to 7, otherwise hit.
3,3	Split on 4 to 7, otherwise hit.
4,4	Never split, always hit.
6,6	Split on 3 to 6, otherwise hit.

Table II
Single Deck Basic Strategy

	Playing Strategy vs.
Your Hand	**Dealer's Upcard**

5,3	Double on 5 or 6, otherwise hit.
9	Double on 2 to 6, otherwise hit.
10	Double on 2 to 9, otherwise hit.
11	Always double.
12	Stand on 4 to 6, otherwise hit.
13 to 16	Stand on 2 to 6, otherwise hit.
17 to 21	Always stand.

A,2 to A,5 . . . Double on 4 to 6, otherwise hit.
A,6 . . . . Double on 2 to 6, otherwise hit.
A,7 . . . . . . Double on 3 to 6. Stand on 2, 7, 8.
                                    Hit on 9, 10 or A.
A,8 . . . . Double on 6, otherwise stand.
A,9 . . . . Always stand.
A,A . . . . Always split.
2,2 . . . . Split on 3 to 7, otherwise hit.
3,3 . . . . Split on 4 to 7, otherwise hit.
4,4 . . . . Same as 8 above.
5,5 . . . . Same as 10 above.
6,6 . . . . Split on 2 to 6, otherwise hit.
7,7 . . . . Split on 2 to 7. Stand on 10.
                                           Otherwise hit.
8,8 . . . . Always split.
9,9 . . . . Split on 2 to 9 except 7.
                                     Stand on 7, 10 or A.
10,10 . . . . Always stand.

The previous chart assumes the casino doesn't allow doubling down after pair splitting. If the casino *allows* doubling down after pair splitting then use the following pair splitting rules.

| | Playing Strategy vs. |
Your Hand	Dealer's Upcard

2,2 . . . . Split on 2 to 7, otherwise hit.
3,3 . . . . Split on 2 to 7, otherwise hit.
4,4 . . . . Split on 4, 5 or 6, otherwise hit.
6,6 . . . . Split on 2 to 7, otherwise hit.
7,7 . Split on 2 to 8. Stand on 10. Otherwise hit.

Table III
Single Deck Basic Strategy
Doubling Down only on 10 and 11

Your Hand	Playing Strategy vs. Dealer's Upcard
8	Always hit.
9	Always hit.
10	Double on 2 to 9, otherwise hit.
11	Double.
12	Stand on 4, 5 or 6, otherwise hit.
13, 14, 15, 16	Stand on 2 to 6, otherwise hit.
17-21	Stand.
A,2 thru A,6	Always hit.
A,7	Stand on 2 to 8, otherwise hit.
A,8 thru A,10	Always stand.
A,A	Split.
2,2	Split on 3 to 7, otherwise hit.
3,3	Split on 4 to 7, otherwise hit.
4,4	Always hit.
5,5	Double on 2 to 9, otherwise hit.
6,6	Split on 2 to 6, otherwise hit.
7,7	Split on 2 to 7. Stand on 10. Otherwise hit.
8,8	Split.
9,9	Split on 2 to 9 except 7. Otherwise stand.
10,10	Stand.

Surrender

In casinos that allow a player to surrender, then surrender the following hands:

Multiple Deck

Your Hand	Dealer's Upcard
16 (except 8,8)	9, 10, Ace
15	10

Do not surrender soft hands

Single Deck

Your Hand	Dealer's Upcard
16 (except 8,8)	10
15	10
7,7	10

Do not surrender soft hands

The above surrender strategy is known as late surrender because players can only surrender after it has been determined that the dealer does not have a blackjack. If a casino allows you to surrender *before* the dealer checks for a blackjack (this is known as early surrender), then use the following early surrender strategy.

Early Surrender Strategy

Dealer's Upcard	Surrender these hands
Ace	5, 6, 7 and 12 thru 17
10	14, 15, 16
9	16 (except 8,8)

Do not surrender soft hands

Early surrender is a very favorable playing option that was once available in all the Atlantic City casinos. Unfortunately, it is rarely offered now but if you're fortunate to find a casino that offers it, be sure to use the above strategy.

Insurance

Whenever the dealer's upcard is an ace, the dealer will ask the players if they wish to make the insurance bet. This is a side bet that a player can make in which he is betting that the dealer's downcard is a ten value card and thus the dealer has a blackjack. Players may make an insurance bet equal to one half of their initial bet. If the dealer has a blackjack, the insurance bets are paid off at 2 to 1. The bottom line, however, is the insurance bet has a high casino advantage and should never be made. Even if you are dealt a blackjack, do *not* make the insurance bet.

Effects of Rule Changes

The following information can be used to estimate the effects various rules have on the casino's advantage. Numbers with a positive sign indicate the percent advantage to the casino. Numbers with a negative sign are player favorable rules.

Single Deck	No Advantage
Two decks	+0.35%
Four decks	+0.52%
Six decks	+0.58%
Eight decks	+0.61%
Dealer hits soft 17	+0.20%
Double on 9, 10 and 11 only	+0.10%
Double on 10 or 11 only	+0.20%
Resplit aces	−0.05%
Double down after splitting	−0.13%
Late surrender	−0.05%
Early surrender	−0.62%
No splitting of aces	+0.17%
Double on 3 or more cards	−0.21%
Six card automatic winner	−0.15%

In addition, you'll find some casinos offering bonus payoffs for a 21 with 7,7,7 or 6,7,8 suited, six cards totaling 21 or less, and others. Some even offer side bets such as betting on whether the dealer's upcard will be red or black, or that the first two player cards will total over or under a 13 total. These side bets have a high casino advantage and should be avoided.

Many casinos have also introduced multiple action blackjack. This game allows players to make three separate wagers on the same hand. After the dealers complete their hand for the first wager, the dealers keep their upcard and complete a second hand against the players original hand. This is repeated a third time to determine the outcome of the third hand. Thus the player's hand is used for three games in which the dealer's upcard remains constant. Casinos are reporting higher win rates at multiple action blackjack tables than regular blackjack tables. The reason is that many players fear "busting" because it results in an immediate loss of three bets, therefore they are abandoning hitting 12 to 16 hands. This violation of basic strategy essentially penalizes the players three times and results in the casinos bigger win rate. Your best bet especially if you are card counting is to play at the traditional blackjack tables.

Card Counting

Once you've mastered the basic strategy you will have reduced the casino's advantage to one half percent or less. You can do even better by learning a skill known as blackjack card counting.

It is beyond the scope of this book to dwell in great detail on the technique of card counting. However, I will review the basics of card counting so that you have an understanding of what it is, how to use it, and why it works.

A large number of computer studies that have been done on card counting all confirm the fact that:

• *Whenever the remaining ratio of cards left to be dealt contains an abundance of ten value cards, the player has the advantage and should make a larger bet size.*

• *Whenever the remaining ratio of cards left to be dealt contains an abundance of low value cards*

(2, 3, 4, 5, 6's), the player is at a disadvantage and should make the minimum bet size.

A card counter keeps track of the ratio of high to low cards by assigning point count values to each card. For example, the low value cards 2, 3, 4, 5, 6, would have a count value of +1. Likewise, the tens, picture cards and aces have the count value of -1. All other cards have a 0 count value.

As the cards are played, the counter arithmetically adds the count value of every card on the table. Thus, if the first player has a 6, 4, 8, the counter's sum is +2. That's because the 6 and 4 each have a +1 value and the 8 has a 0 count value. Adding the +1 to the +1 the sum is +2. If the next player shows a jack and 7, the point value of these cards (which are -1 and 0) must be added to the +2. The net sum is +1 (+2+[-1]= +1). In this manner, the counter continues to add the +1's and -1's until the round is completed. When this occurs, the counter has either a plus number or minus number or perhaps 0 as the arithmetic sum. The latter is known as the running count. And if the running count is positive, it means the player has the advantage on the next deal.

Likewise, if the running count is negative, the dealer now has the advantage. The more positive the running count, the greater is the player's advantage and the larger should be the bet size.

A suggested bet size based upon the running count is as follows:

Single Deck Game

Running Count	Bet Size
Negative to +1	1 unit[2]
+2	2 units
+3	3 units
+4 or more	4 units

Multiple Deck Game

Running Count	Bet Size
0 to +3	1 unit
+4 to +6	2 units
+7 to +9	3 units
+10 or more	4 units

If you follow the basic playing strategy and size your bets based upon the running count, you will now join an elite group of skillful casino players that have the advantage over the casino. In other words, over the long run, you can't lose.

Practice card counting at home by taking a deck of cards and flip them over one at a time. As you see each card, keep the running count. You will know you are keeping an accurate count if your final count after going through a deck of cards totals 0. Keep practicing until you can accurately count down a single deck of cards in about 30 seconds.

---

[2]If your minimum bet is $5.00, then $5.00 represents 1 unit. $10.00 would be 2 units and so forth.

There are other refinements to card counting which can be learned once the basics are mastered. These include true count wagering, how to act in a casino to prevent from being barred from play, team play and more. But walk before you run - start first by mastering bet sizing based upon the running count.

Blackjack Playing Rules

The following playing rules are in effect in the Atlantic City casinos. Blackjack playing rules in other casinos may differ slightly.

Objective: To beat the dealer by having your cards total higher than his cards, without your cards going over 21.

Card Values: The cards from 2 through 10 count face value. All picture cards count ten. The ace counts as 1 or 11 at the player's discretion.

Mechanics: The minimum bet is $2 to $3 (varies from casino to casino). There are also $5, $10, $25 and higher minimum bet tables. Chips can be obtained at the table. All cards are dealt from a shoe by the dealer. You will receive two cards - face up - and the dealer will have one card face-up and one face-down. The dealer will not reveal his hole or face-down card until all players have completed their hands. The dealer must take an extra card if he has 16 or less, and continue doing so until he has at least 17. The dealer must stand with his hand if he has more than 17.

Player Options:

Hit: Request another card. Give a hand signal by scratching index finger on table.

Stand: Satisfied with hand - no more cards. Give hand signal by waving hand over cards.

Double Down: Double your bet by putting the same amount next to first bet. BUT, you only receive ONE more card. This can be done with any two card hand.

Pair Splitting: Any two identical value cards can be split and played as two separate hands. As many additional cards as you wish may be drawn to each "split hand," EXCEPT a pair of aces. Only one card is drawn to each split ace. Signal for pair splitting is to place an amount of chips equal to your original bet next to your original bet in the betting area.

Insurance: When the dealer has an ace showing, (that means facing up) he will request Insurance. A player may make an Insurance bet equal to one half (1/2) of the original bet. You win the Insurance bet at a 2 to 1 payoff if the dealer has BLACKJACK.

Additional Rules:

- Doubling down is permitted after splitting a pair.

- Pair splitting a third time is permitted.

- A blackjack hand beats a 21 hand. Blackjack is a two-card 21 in which the first two cards dealt must equal 21.

- If a player doubles down or pair splits and the dealer ends up having blackjack, only the original wager is lost-the extra wager made in doubling down or pair splitting is returned to the player.

- A player's blackjack pays 3 to 2. All hands higher than the dealer's total at the end win at 1 to 1. All hands less than the dealer's total at the end lose. If the player's and dealer's hands total the same, this is a tie (called a push) and no chips are exchanged. The dealer signals this by tapping the table.

- Remember never to touch the cards or your bet until the hand is won or pushed. Then you can pick up your chips.

- The surrender option was recently reinstated in the Atlantic City casinos. This option allows the player to give up the opportunity to play out the hand in return for forfeiting one-half of the initial wager.

Best Bet #2
PASS LINE/
COME WITH ODDS

The second best bet in a casino is located on the craps table. It is the pass line with odds bet. It has almost the same casino advantage as the don't pass bet, which is our third best bet.

The majority of craps players will wager on the pass line rather than the don't pass line. The reason for this will become clear in a moment.

Because the pass line is so popular, the betting area for making this bet runs all around the layout. So no matter where you stand, you can easily make this bet.

You must make your wager on the pass line prior to the initial roll of a shooter (or dice thrower). This first roll is known as the come-out roll and you'll always know when it's a come-out roll by observing the position of the ON/OFF disc located at the top of the layout. If the disc shows ON and is located in a box with a number 4, 5, 6, 8, 9, or 10, then the next roll is NOT a come-out roll. You should wait until the game in progress is over, at which time the dealer will turn the disc (sometimes called a puck) over to the OFF position and place it in the DON'T COME area of the layout. If you see this, then and only then should you make your pass line wager.

If the come-out throw is a 7 or 11 (known as naturals), you win the pass line bet. If instead a 2, 3 or 12 appears, you lose.

If the shooter establishes a point, then the pass line bet is won if the shooter repeats the point number before tossing a 7. If, on the other hand, a 7 appears before the point number, then the pass line bet loses.

All winning pass line bets are paid off at 1 to 1. If you bet $5 and you win, the payoff is the same, or $5.

A bet on the pass line has a casino advantage of 1.41%. We can reduce this casino advantage by making the odds bet.

You make the odds bet once a point number is established. If you had a $5 wager on the pass line and the point was 6, you would put $5 in odds to win $6.

The payoff for a winning pass line odds bet is always more than the initial odds bet. The exact payoff depends on what the point number is.

Point	Odds Payoff
4/10	2 to 1
5/9	3 to 2
6/8	6 to 5

The above tells you that if the point was 4 or 10, the odds payoff is 2 chips for every 1 chip bet. Likewise, for the point numbers 5 or 9, the payoff is 3 to 2 and for the 6 or 8 it's 6 to 5.

Let us go through an example. You make a $5 bet on the pass line and the shooter establishes 10 as the point. You now place an additional $5 in chips directly *behind* your pass line wager (this is the odds bet). If the shooter repeats the 10 before tossing a 7, you win your pass line bet and the odds bet. The $5 pass line bet pays $5 (1 to 1 payoff). The $5 odds bet pays $10 (2 to 1 payoff).

Of course, if the shooter threw a 7 instead of repeating the point number, then both bets, the pass line and the odds bet, would be lost.

In the above example, the amount of your odds bet was equal to the pass line bet. This is known as single odds. The latter will reduce the casino advantage from 1.41% to 0.85%.

A casino that allows double odds means the player can wager twice as much on odds. A $5 pass line bet could be covered with a $10 odds bet. Likewise, triple odds allows a $15 odds bet for an initial $5 pass line bet.

The following chart summarizes the odds bet and pass line bet for single, double or triple odds.

PROPER ODDS BET*

Point	Pass Line	Single	Double	Triple
4/10	$5	$5(10)	$10(20)	$15(30)
5/9	$5	6(9)	10(15)	18(27)
6/8	$5	5(6)	10(12)	15(18)

*Payoffs in parenthesis

The casino advantage for the pass line bet with single, double or triple odds is as follows:

Pass line	1.41%
Pass line with single odds	0.85%
Pass line with double odds	0.67%
Pass line with triple odds	0.47%

Some casinos allow five and even ten times odds. This reduces the casino's advantage to 0.32 and 0.18% respectively.

The odds bet is an excellent bet for the player because the casino advantage is so low. Remember - the lower the casino advantage, the better are your chances of winning the bet.

A similar bet to the pass line is the come bet. Once a point is established, you can make a come bet. The bet wins if the next dice throw is a 7 or 11. It loses if a 2, 3 or 12 appears. If instead the shooter throws a 4, 5, 6, 8, 9 or 10, then the dealer will pick up your come bet and put it into the point box at the top of the layout. You may now make the odds bet by putting chips in the come betting area and telling the dealer to "put odds on the 10 (or whatever point number was thrown)." The dealer will pick up your odds bet and put them on top of, but slightly off center, the initial come bet. You win this bet (come plus odds) if the shooter repeats the come point number before tossing a 7. You lose if the 7 appears before the come-point number. It is always assumed that the odds bet for a come point are off or not working on all come-out rolls to establish the shooters point.

Summary   I would recommend that you confine your bets to the pass line with odds to begin with. Once you feel comfortable making these bets, then you might want to try one come bet with odds. Do not wager more than the pass line with odds and two come bets with odds. This should be a sufficient amount of bets on the table to profit from a shooter who throws numbers other than the 7.

If you are playing single odds, you'll get the maximum odds if you wager 3 units on the pass line and take 3 units odds on 4/10, 4 units odds on 5/9, and 5 units odds on 6/8. For double odds, make your initial pass line bet 2 units with 4 units odds on 4, 5, 9, 10 and 5 units on 6 and 8. If you can take five times or higher odds, make your pass line wager as low as possible (ideally, $1) then take the maximum odds.[3] Remember that when making an odds bet on 5 or 9, it should be made in even multiples (because of the 3 to 2 payoff) and odds on 6 or 8 should be made in multiples of 5 (6 to 5 payoff). If not sure, ask the dealer for help on making the correct odds bets.

---

[3]An alternate more conservative playing strategy is to start wagering with only single odds, then as you win, gradually increase the odds bet to double, triple, etc. (keeping the pass line wager the same). Once you lose a bet, start again with single odds.

Best Bet #3
DON'T PASS/
DON'T COME WITH ODDS

Best bet #3 is also located on the craps table. It is one of the basic craps bets that has a low casino advantage of only 0.5 to 0.8% making it the third best bet in the casino.

Let us first concentrate on the don't pass bet.

There is an area on the craps table layout clearly marked DON'T PASS BAR 12 (or 2). This is where you place your wager on the don't pass.

Like the pass line wager, you must wait to make the don't pass bet until the come-out roll. When the puck is in the OFF position, it is time to place your chips on the don't pass line.

The rules for winning and losing a don't pass bet are as follows. You win if the shooter throws a 2 or 3 on the come-out roll. You lose if instead a 7 or 11 is thrown. If a 12 is thrown, the don't pass bet is pushed or tied (you don't win or lose). This is why you see BAR 12 on the layout.

If the shooter throws a 4, 5, 6, 8, 9 or 10 on the come-out roll, then the rules for winning or losing change. The number thrown is known as the shooter's point. The shooter must now continue to throw the dice until one of two events occur. If the shooter throws a 7 before throwing the point number, then you win your don't pass bet. If instead, the shooter throws the point number instead of a 7, then the don't pass wager is lost.

Let us try some sample dice throws to be sure you understand these rules. Assume the dice throws were as follows: 4, 6, 9, 11, 3, 7. Four was thrown on the come-out roll and is the shooter's point. The next toss was a 6. This has no consequence on our bet. Likewise, the 9, 11 and 3 have no bearing. The sixth toss gives us a 7. Since the 7 was thrown before a second four (the point number), then the don't pass bettor wins. A winning don't pass bet pays 1 to 1 which means if you wager $5 you win $5. (Note: In the example even though don't pass bettors win, players betting on pass line lose).

Example: 3, 6, 5, 6, 2, 11. The first toss was a 3. This is an automatic win for the don't pass bettor. The next come-out roll was a 6. This was followed by a 5 and another 6. Since the 6 repeated, the don't pass bettor loses. The next come-out roll was a 2. This gives the don't pass bettor a win. However, the next come-out roll was an 11, which results in a loss.

When you make a don't pass bet, the casino's advantage is 1.4%. But we can lower the 1.4% casino advantage to 0.5 to 0.8% by laying odds along with the don't pass bet.

Let's assume you make the don't pass wager. The come-out roll is 10, establishing 10 as the point. Now you may make the odds bet. How much you should wager in odds depends upon the point number.

Point	Don't Pass Bet	Odds Bet
4/10	$5	$10
5/9	$5	$ 9
6/8	$5	$ 6

You win your odds bet just like the don't pass bet, namely when the shooter throws a 7 before repeating the point number. The winning payoff depends upon the point number. The payoff is 1 to 2 for the point numbers 4 and 10; 2 to 3 for the point numbers 5 and 9; and 5 to 6 on the point numbers 6 and 8. What this means is that if, for example, you wager $10 in odds when the point is 4, you'd win $5 (1 to 2 payoff) if the shooter throws a 7 before a 4.

The odds bet payoff is always less than the odds bet because the player has the advantage over the casino once a point is established. The number 7 which is a winner for the don't pass bettor once a point is established, can be thrown in more ways with a pair of dice than any other number. This is why the don't pass bettor is a favorite once a point is established and it's also why you must bet more to win less. The latter is one of the main reasons why the majority of craps players play the pass line vs. don't pass.

There are casinos that offer single, double,

triple, or more odds. Single odds means the size of your odds wager must be such that if it wins, the payoff should equal the size of the don't pass bet. If $5 is wagered on don't pass and the point is 6, the proper odds bet is $6, since the odds payoff would be $5 (equal to original don't pass line bet). If the point were 10, a $5 don't pass line bet would take a $10 odds bet. (The latter would yield a $5 payoff if it won).

By taking single odds along with your don't pass bet, the casino's advantage for the combined don't pass plus single odds is only 0.8%. This makes this the #3 best bet in the casino.

The casino's advantage could be lowered even further by making a double or triple odds bet. If you make a don't pass wager in a casino that allows double odds, then the size of the odds wager could be such that the odds payoff is twice the original don't pass bet. If the point was 10 and you had a $5 don't pass bet, you would be allowed to make a maximum double odds bet of $20 to win $10 (1 to 2 payoff). Note the payoff for the winning odds bet ($10) is twice the amount ($5) of the original don't pass bet.

The same rules hold for triple odds, only here your winning odds payoff could equal three times the original don't pass bet.

Double odds will reduce the casino's advantage to 0.6% and triple odds reduces it to slightly less than 0.5%.

Here is a chart summarizing the odds bet and payoffs for a typical $5 bet.

Proper Odds Bet*

Don't Pass Bet	Point Number	Single	Double	Triple
$5	4/10	$10(5)	$20(10)	$30(15)
$5	5/9	9(6)	15(10)	27(18)
$5	6/8	6(5)	12(10)	18(15)

*Payoffs in parentheses

I would recommend you begin playing the don't pass with single odds. If you don't know how much to wager in odds, simply ask the dealer and they will tell you the correct amount. Watch also how the dealer positions the odds bet on the table. The chips are placed next to the original don't pass bet. In dealer's parlance, sometimes the chips are bridged, other times healed. Don't let these terms frighten you...simply put the chips you wish to wager in odds next to the original don't pass bet and the dealer will stack your chips properly. Watch how they do it and then do the same each time you make the odds bet.

There is another bet on the craps table similar to the don't pass bet with odds. It is known as the don't come bet, and it has the same low casino advantage as the don't pass bet.

You make the don't pass bet on the come-out roll. The don't come bet is made on all other rolls of the dice. It is an independent bet but has the same win and lose rules as the don't pass bet.

Once a shooter establishes a point number, a player may wager in the don't come. If the next throw is 2 or 3, the don't come bet is won. If instead, it's a 7 or 11, it loses. If the next toss is instead a 4, 5, 6, 8, 9, or 10, then the don't come bet is physically moved by the dealer from the don't come area to the top of the don't come point box. A player can make the odds bet by putting the correct number of chips in the don't come area, and telling the dealer loud and clear, "put odds on my 4 (or whatever point number)." The dealer will pick-up the odds bet and position them next to the don't come bet.

If you are a beginner, get your feet wet by making the don't pass bet with odds first. After you become confident on how to make this bet, you then might want to try the don't come bet for some extra action.

Summary   The third best bet in a casino is the don't pass (and don't come) bet with odds. Triple and double odds reduces the casino's advantage even more than the single odds, but as a beginner, test the waters first by learning how to make a don't pass bet with single odds.

Best Bet #4 & #5
Bank Hand/Player Hand

The fourth and fifth best casino bets can be found on the baccarat tables.

Baccarat is an elegant European casino game that is played in a secluded, confined area of the casino known as the baccarat pit. The decor of the "pit" is one of splendor. The game is dealt by dealers wearing tuxedos and the environment is calm and peaceful. To the average gamer, the baccarat pit appears to be a socially quarantined area where you need to know someone in order to play. This is, of course, not true and the game of baccarat is open to anyone. Unfortunately, not too many tourists enter the pit because of the complicated-appearing layout, the games reputation of being "only for high rollers," and the awesomeness of it all. Nevertheless, baccarat is an exciting and simple game that offers the player the fourth and fifth best bet in a casino.

Baccarat tables generally seat 14 players and the table layout clearly indicates where each player must place their wager. The minimum bet requirements for each table are posted. Most offer $5 and $20 minimum bet games.

The object of the game is to guess which of two hands will win. The two hands are known as the bank hand and player hand. Cards are dealt to each hand and the hand whose total is closest to 9 is the winner.

Eight decks of cards are used in baccarat and the value of the cards is as follows: all picture cards and tens count zero and the ace thru nine count face value. For example, a 2 and 3 equals a baccarat hand of 5. A jack and 9 totals 9, and an ace and ten equal 1.

In baccarat, a hand can never exceed nine points, so totals over nine are adjusted by subtracting ten. For example, an $8 + 9 = 7$ (not 17); $8 + 5 = 3$; $6 + 6 = 2$.

At the start of a game, all players are requested to make their bets on either the bank hand or player hand to win. You place your wager in the betting area marked bank or player directly in front of you. A third bet is available, known as the tie bet, and here a player wagers that the bank and player hand will have the same total. These three bets are the only ones allowed.

In baccarat, the players must deal the cards. Every player has an opportunity to deal and the shoe containing the cards will rotate counterclockwise around the table. A player may refuse to deal, in which case the shoe is offered to the next player.

To deal the cards in baccarat, you must slide

one card face down to the caller (the name of the dealer who controls the pace of the game), the second card face down under the front corner of the shoe, the third card is given face down to the caller and the fourth tucked under the shoe with the second card.

The two cards in front of the caller represent the player hand and the two cards tucked under the shoe represent the bank hand.

The caller will give the player cards to that player who has the highest wager on the player hand. This player looks at the cards and tosses them back to the caller who announces the total of the two cards. For example, "players have 2." The caller now asks for the bank cards and the player who dealt removes the two bank hand cards from under the corner of the shoe, faces the cards, and tosses them to the caller who announces the bank hand total.

In baccarat, a two card total of either 8 or 9 is known as a natural. If either the bank or player hand two cards total 8 or 9, the game is over and the hand with the higher total is declared the winner. All winning wagers are paid off at 1 to 1.

In the event neither the player or bank hand totals 8 or 9, then there are specific rules which determine if these hands draw a third card or not. It is not necessary to memorize these third card rules since the caller is responsible for determining the card totals and will request a third card draw as required. Nevertheless, you will enjoy the game better if you have some familiarization with these rules.

Player Hand Third Card Rules

The sole variable which determines whether or not the player hand should receive a third card is the *total* of the two card player hand. If the total is 0 thru 5, then the player hand receives a third card. If instead, the player hand totals, 6, 7, 8, 9 then the hand cannot draw. For example 7 + 3 = 0 (draws); 9 + 8 = 7 (stands); Q + K = 0 (draws). Notice the total of the bank hand has no bearing on whether or not the player hand draws.

Bank Hand Third Card Rules

These rules are different and a little more complex. Here there are two variables which determine whether or not the bank hand draws. They are 1) the total of the two card bank hand and in some instances 2) the value of the third card drawn by the player hand. If the bank hand totals 0, 1, 2 then the bank hand must draw a third card. If the hand totals 7, 8, 9 then bank hand must stand.

If the bank hand totals 3, 4, 5 or 6 then the rules for drawing are as follows.

Bank 2 Card Total	Bank hand draws when players third card is	Bank hand stands when players third card is
3	0,1,2,3,4,5,6,7,9	8
4	2,3,4,5,6,7	0,1,8,9
5	4,5,6,7	0,1,2,3,8,9
6	6,7	0,1,2,3,4,5,8,9

In the event the player hand stands on two cards, then the two card bank hands totaling 3, 4, 5 must draw and 6 must stand.

Let's try an example. You wager $5 on the bank hand and the initial two card hands are: player-4, J; bank-2, Ace. Player hand always goes first. The hand totals 4. By the rules the hand must draw. Assume the draw card is an 8. Player's final total is 4, J, 8 = 2. The initial two card bank hand was 3 (2 + ace). By the rules the bank hand total of 3 must stand when the player third card draw was an 8. The result of this game is the bank hand beat the player hand "3 over 2" and thus you win $5.

Based on a mathematical analysis of the game, it has been determined that the bank hand will win 45.8% of the time, player hand 44.6% and tie 9.6%. **If we discount the hands that result in a tie,** we discover that the bank hand stands to win 50.7% of the time and player hand 49.3%. Notice that the bank hand wins greater than 50% of the time which means if you bet bank you would have the edge over the casino. Since the casinos are not in business to give players the advantage, they compensate for this advantage on the bank hand by charging a 5% commission every time you win a bank hand bet. Thus, if you bet $20 on bank hand and it wins, you will be paid $20 and the dealer will place a $1 marker in your commission box located in the center of the layout. At the end of play or when the shoe is completed, you are expected to pay the casino the total amount of commissions owed.

The fact that you must pay this 5% commission only on winning bank hand bets doesn't mean its a bad bet. Even by taking into consideration this commission, the calculation of the casino's advantage or percent over the player is 1.17% for bank hand; 1.36% for player hand; 14.1% for tie bet. The tie bet should be avoided as the casino's advantage is much too high.

Many casinos also offer a lower stakes baccarat game called mini-baccarat. The game is played on a blackjack size table in the main casino as opposed to the regular baccarat game which usually is set aside in a special playing area. The rules for mini-baccarat are the same as regular baccarat. It is an excellent way to play baccarat as a beginner for low stakes.

Summary Both the bank and player hand bets are smart bets because they have a relatively low casino advantage. The bank hand's casino advantage is 1.17% and the player hand is 1.36%.

Best Bet #6
PLACE BETS ON 6 AND 8

The sixth best casino bet is the craps place bets on the 6 and 8.

Craps players are permitted at any time to make a bet that the 6 and 8 will appear when the dice are tossed before a 7. The most popular way of making this kind of bet is to "place" the numbers.

First, let me go through the mechanics of making this bet. Assume for the moment you've stepped up to the craps table and you want to make a wager on the number 6. In order to make this bet, you must put your chips on the table in the area labeled, "Come," get the dealer's attention and say "Place the six." The dealer will put your chips in the lower part of the 6 numbered box at the top of the layout. In Atlantic City, there is a special area within the box for place bets (you'll see the word "place" written on the layout).

The important thing to remember about making place bets is that these bets must be made by the dealer. You never put chips in the point box numbers at the top of the layout-only the dealer is permitted to place player bets in this area.

So, you've made a place bet on the 6. Now what happens? Well, if the shooter throws the dice and a 6 appears before he throws a 7, you win the bet. On the other hand, if a 7 appears before the 6, you lose the bet.

For example, if the dice numbers after you made your place 6 bet were 3, 2, 9, 11, 6 you'd win the bet (note that the 6 appeared before a 7). If instead, the dice rolls were 9, 2, 12, 7 you'd lose the bet.

When you make place bets on the 6 or 8, you must bet in multiples of six dollars in order to get the maximum odds payoffs. The place bet on the 6 and 8 pay 7 to 6. Thus, your minimum bet should be $6 to win $7.

Now how about our chances of winning? In order to calculate this, we must compare our true odds for winning the bet vs. the casino payoff. For example, the number 6 can be rolled in five different dice combinations (5,1; 1,5; 2,4; 4,2; 3,3), whereas the 7 can be rolled in six ways (1,6; 6,1; 2,5; 5,2; 3,4; 4,3). Now when we make a place bet on the number 6, we're hoping that the shooter throws a 6 before a 7. The chances are 6 to 5 against this happening. Therefore, the risk you take when you make this bet is 6 to 5, yet the casino payoff if you win is not 6 to 5, but rather 7 to 6. Notice the casino has paid you less then the risk you took when you made the bet. This difference represents the casino's advantage and in mathematical terms this works out to 1.51%, which makes this bet the sixth best bet in the casino.

A few more items you should know when you place the 6 or 8: these bets can be taken off or removed from the table anytime you want to do so. Also, these bets are automatically off (or not working) on the come-out roll (the dice roll that established the point). And when you win a place bet, the dealer will only give you your winnings ($7) and the original $6 bet will remain on the layout. If you want that back too, simply tell the dealer to "take down the six."

With a 1.5% casino advantage, the 6 and 8 place bets are smart bets to make on the craps table and the intelligent bettor will learn to use these bets to maximize profits on "hot rolls."

Best Bet #7
VIDEO POKER

Enough research has been done in recent years to make playing the video poker machines one of the ten best bets in the casino. But you must know how to play each hand correctly and learn which machines to play. If you do this then it's possible to reduce the casino's advantage to 3% or less (in fact you may even be able to reduce the advantage to 0 or actually have a slight edge over the casino).

Video poker machines work as follows. A player places a coin or coins (most machines take more than one coin) into the machine, pulls the handle or pushes a button that states "deal," and presto five cards appear on the display screen. The player must now decide how many of these five cards should be kept and which ones to discard. This is accomplished by pushing the draw or hold button located under each card. The object, of course, is to improve your hand in order to get the highest poker hand possible. The higher the hand, the greater the payoff.

In the majority of casinos, there are generally two types of poker machines - those that pay with a minimum of jacks or better and those that require at least 2 pair. Some machines use a joker as a wild card, others a deuce. We'll concentrate on the more popular video poker machines without a wild card.

Playing video poker on a machine is not quite the same as playing in a regular table game. You don't raise and you can't bluff. And you must play every hand. But playing poker on a machine does have certain advantages. The stakes are low (25 cents per game). You never have to be concerned about getting into a "shady" game. And like the regular table game, skillful players have a much better chance of winning on these machines than the non-skilled. This is what makes video poker a lot better buy than playing the regular slot machines where skill is not much of a factor.

Video Poker is a game of skill and it's important to know which machine to play and how to play your hands.

The first rule to becoming a skillful player is to only play machines that return your bet if you have jacks or better (rather than two pair). From time to time, casinos offer machines that pay on tens or better which is an even better bet for the player.

Next, look at the payoff schedule on the machine. If you are playing a non-progressive video poker machine, you want to play on a machine that has at least a 4,000 coin payout for a 5 coin royal flush, and pays 9 coins for a one coin full house and 6 coins for a flush. These are known as 9-6 machines and they are a much better play than machines that pay less than 9 for the full house or 6 for the flush. It's up to you to find these 9-6 machines with at least a 4,000 coin payout for a royal flush. They are available so don't settle for a lower paying machine.

If you are playing a progressive video poker machine, the normal full house/flush payout for one coin is 8-5. On these machines, the payout for a royal flush continually grows.

Play only on machines that pay at least $2200 (for 25 cent machine) for a royal flush.

Now that you know which machines to play, you must learn how to play your hands. Here are some tips:

    1. Never keep a kicker. If you have a pair of anything or 3 of a kind, don't keep a kicker.

    2. Don't discard all five cards if you have one or two cards higher than 10 and the machine pays off on pairs of J, Q, K, aces.

    3. Be aggressive in trying for the royal flush. Draw one card to a royal flush even if you have to break up a straight, pair, or flush. You should always draw two cards to a royal flush with two exceptions--if you have a pair of jacks or better or you need one card for a straight flush.

    4. Always draw one card for a straight flush even if it means breaking up a pair.

    5. Always draw one card for a flush except if you hold a pair, it's better to draw three to the pair (on machines that pay on pairs). If you are

playing on a machine that does not pay off on pairs, then always draw to the flush.

6. Draw one card for a straight if the card you need is for an open end straight.

7. Always draw three cards to a small pair-don't keep the kicker!

8. Do not draw one card to an inside straight. You are better off holding your high card or cards and drawing 3 or 4 cards.

9. Never break up a full house or four of a kind.

10. If you are dealt five odd cards, keep four card straights and flushes, keep two cards (or more) for a royal flush, and if you have none of the above, keep one jack or higher and discard the rest.

If you follow the above rules and select the correct payoff machines, you'll have lowered the casino's advantage to less than 3%. In fact, if the royal flush payoff gets very high, you can actually have the edge over the casinos. Now that's a smart bet for any player.

For further information on how to make the correct playing decision for every possible poker hand, I recommend you consult the following books: *Expert Video Poker* by Lenny Frome and *Professional Video Poker* by Stanford Wong.

Best Bet #8
4 AND 10 LAY BET

The 4 and 10 lay bet is not a very common craps bet because it generally requires a minimum wager of $40. Still, it's a smart bet because of its low casino advantage (2.4%). And if you can afford to make this kind of bet, you should consider it. In fact, I'll show you a nice technique of how to use this bet as an insurance bet in conjunction with a don't pass line bet.

A player can make a lay bet on any of the point numbers (4, 5, 6, 8, 9 or 10). If a player makes a lay bet on the 4, he is betting that the 7 will show before the 4. If it does he wins the bet. If instead, the 4 appears before a 7, he loses the lay bet.

The payoff on a 4 or 10 lay bet is 1 to 2. This means you are paid an amount of chips equal to one-half the original bet. If you make a $40 lay bet on the 10, and you win, you would be paid $20.

When you make a lay bet, you must pay the casino a commission or vigorish. This commission is 5% of the amount of payoff you would receive if the bet won. Thus, in the previous example, a player would put $41 in the don't come area of the layout and announce to the dealer, $40 no 4." The dealer will put the chips behind the numbered box 4 and cap the chips with a "buy" button. The leftover $1 chip representing the 5% of $20 commission is kept by the dealer (put into casino chip tray).

Since most casinos charge a minimum commission of $1 (representing one white chip), it stands to reason that the minimum lay bet on the 4 or 10 should be $40 (since the payoff is $20 and 5% of $20 is $1). The majority of casinos also allow a $50 wager to win $25 and still collect only a $1 commission. This will reduce the casino advantage to 2.0%.

Lay bets are always working, even on come-out rolls. They can also be removed by the player at any time. To do so, simply announce to the dealer to "take down my $40 lay bet on 4." The dealer will return the $40 plus $1 commission to you.

Here's how we can use the 4 or 10 lay bet as an insurance bet.

You know that the throw of a seven on the come-out roll spells disaster for the don't pass bettor. Therefore, after making the don't pass bet on the come-out roll, immediately put $41 on the table and tell the dealer "$40 no 4." The dealer will put your $40 lay bet in the top of the 4 come box and cap it with a buy button. The extra $1 is kept as a commission. Thus, you have two bets on the layout prior to the come-out throw-your don't pass bet and the lay bet on the 4. The latter bet *wins* if the shooter throws a 7 before a 4. Thus, if the shooter throws a 7 on the come-out roll, you'll lose your don't pass bet, but will win the lay bet on the 4. The latter pays 1 to 2 so you win $20 for the $40 bet. You only make the lay bet for one roll-if the shooter establishes a point on the come-out, then you immediately tell the dealer to take down your $40 lay bet. He'll return the $40 plus $1 commissions to you. A very nice one roll insurance bet to help you neutralize those come-out 7's.

Best Bet #9
PAI GOW POKER

Pai gow poker, also known as Asian poker, is a cross between Pai Gow, the game of Chinese dominoes, and the American game of seven-card poker. It is an easy game to play and it's unique since it allows the player the option to bank bets against all other players, including the dealer.

Pai gow poker is played using a standard 52-card deck plus one joker on a table similar to a blackjack table. The layout allows up to six players and one casino dealer. After the players make their bets, the casino dealer will deal out seven cards to each player. Each player must arrange his seven cards into two hands. One hand, called the low hand, consists of two cards. The other hand, called the high hand, consists of the remaining five cards.

Card rankings are based on basic poker rankings. The joker is a special card - not a wildcard as it can be used only as an ace or as a card to complete a straight, a flush, a straight flush, or a royal flush. The objective of the game is to form a high hand and a low hand that are both higher in rank than the respective hands of the dealer.

All pai gow poker hands are ranked according to traditional poker rankings. For example, the highest two-card low hand is a pair of aces. The highest-ranking five card high hand is five aces (four aces plus the joker). A straight-flush hand would beat a full house and a straight beats three-of-a-kind. A complete listing of the pai gow poker hand rankings can be found at the end of this chapter.

The following is a basic description of the pai gow poker rules.

The casino dealer shuffles the 53 cards, which are then cut by a player using a cut card. All players must place their gaming chips on the appropriate betting area of the layout and the dealer will then announce "no more bets."

A dice shaker containing three dice is used to determine who receives the first hand. The casino dealer will shake the dice cup, remove the lid, and announce the total of the three dice. The position of the dealer is number one. The playing position to the right of the dealer is number two, the next position is three continuing counterclockwise around the table. The casino dealer's position is always considered number one, eight and 15. Keep in mind that all six player positions are used in the counting process whether or not a player is actually seated and playing (all empty and full player positions are counted). If the three-dice total is 14, the sixth wagering position (first player position to the left of the dealer) would receive the first card.

Once the determination is made as to who receives the first card, the dealer will deal the cards face down to each player position so that each player and the dealer receives seven cards. The dealer will remove the cards from those player positions where there is no wager and then check that there are four undealt cards left (indicating a valid deal).

The players may then pick up their cards and arrange the cards into two-card low hand and five-card high hand.

It is very important to remember that the five-card high hand must be higher in rank than the two-card low hand, otherwise it results in an automatic losing hand. For example, if the player's two-card hand contains a pair of 5s and the five-card hand contains only a pair of 3s, the hand was not set correctly and automatically loses. In this particular example, if the two-card hand contains a pair of 5s, the five-card hand must contain as least a pair of 6s or higher in order to be arranged properly.

This is the most important rule to remember when playing pai gow poker: The five-card hand must be higher than the two-card hand.

Each player is responsible for arranging his cards into the best high and low hands. Once this is done, the players place their two hands face down on the appropriate area of the layout (the two-card low hand is placed closest to the dealer, and the five-card high hand is placed behind the low hand and closer to the player).

After all the players have set their hands and placed them on the layout, the dealer will turn over his seven cards and set them into a low and high hand. There are specific house rules that the dealer must follow to set his hands. Once the dealer sets his cards into low and high hands, the dealer then turns over the cards of each of the players' hands and compares the rank of each to the dealer's high and low hands.

In order to win your wager, your low hand and high hand must both rank higher than the dealer's low and high hands. If one of your hands is higher in rank than the dealer's and the other is lower, this is a tie and your bet remains on the layout (e.g. your high hand beats the dealer's high hand but his low hand beats your low hand). A tie also occurs if one of your hands is identical in rank to the dealer's hand (this is known as a copy hand) and the other hand is higher than the dealer's respective hand. A player will lose his or her wager under the following situations:

1) Both player hands are lower in rank than the dealer's respective hands.

2) Both player hands are copy hands.

3) One player hand is a copy hand and the other hand is lower in rank than the dealer's respective hands.

4) The player's high hand was set incorrectly and does not rank higher than his low hand.

5) The player does not set the hands properly; for example, he forms a three-card low

hand and a four-card high hand.

Once the dealer has determined if a player hand wins, loses or is a push, the dealer will collect all losing wagers, leave all tie wagers on the layout and pay off all winning wagers at 1-to-1 (if you bet $5 you win $5). In pai gow poker, the casino collects a 5 percent commission (or vigorish) from all winning hands. This commission is collected by the dealer at the time of the winning payoff. Thus if you bet $5 and won, the dealer will give you $5 for your win but you must then give the dealer 25 cents (5 percent commission). You do not pay any commission if your bet loses or ties.

Each casino at its discretion may offer to all players the opportunity to "bank" the game. Each player, in turn starting from the dealer's right, has the option to be the bank or pass the bank to the next player (counterclockwise). If a player accepts to be the bank, a marker will be placed in front of this player. If no player accepts to be the banker, then the dealer will assume that role.

There are specific rules that casinos use regarding a player who wants to be the banker. For example, in order to be the banker, the player must have placed a wager against the dealer during the last round of play in which there was no player banking the game.

Also, the player must have sufficient gaming chips on the table to cover all of the wagers placed by other players at the table for that round. And in some casinos, the player is not allowed to bank two consecutive rounds of play.

When a player acts as the banker, all other player hands are compared to the banker's hand and not to the dealer's. The player acting as banker gets to shake the dice cup and is counted as position one for determining who will be dealt the first card. When a player banks, the dealer will wager an amount equal to the player's bet on the preceding hand. The banker has the option, however, to request that the dealer wager a lesser amount or not wager during that round of play. Also, when a player banks, all losing wagers are immediately collected and placed in the center of the table. The dealer will use these gaming chips to pay off winning wagers. If there are not enough chips, the banker must make up the difference. Likewise, all chips left after the round is completed are given to the banker after the dealer collects the 5 percent commission based upon the amount left.

A word of caution should another player act as banker: Be very careful not to expose your hand since the banker would have a distinct advantage if he knew what your hand is prior to setting his or her hand.

As a general rule, a player who bets as the banker has a slight edge over the rest of the players because in the event that both hands are copy hands, the banker wins.

Another option available to the player who acts as banker is to request that the casino cover 50 percent of the wagers made during a round of play (so called co-banking). When a player acting as banker requests co-banking, then the banker cards must be set according to established house rules from the two hands.

A casino may, at its discretion, allow a player to wager on two adjacent betting areas. If a player wagers different amounts on two adjacent hands, the player must rank and set the hand with the larger wager before he or she is allowed to rank and set the other hand.

Another unique rule is that a player may surrender his wager after the hands of the dealer have been set. The player must announce his intention to surrender prior to the dealer exposing either of the two hands of the player. When a player surrenders, he will automatically lose the wager. Note: When a player surrenders, the entire bet is lost, not 50 percent of the bet.

Then why surrender at all? Because traditionally in pai gow, it is considered preferable to surrender rather than endure the humiliation of the dealer exposing a player's poor hand.

Pai Gow Poker Hand Rankings:

Five aces - four aces and joker.

Royal flush - ace, queen, king, jack and 10 of the same suit.

Straight flush - five consecutive-ranked cards in any suit as 10, 9, 8, 7, 6 of hearts - the highest straight-flush hand is ace, 2, 3, 4, 5; the second highest is K, Q, J, 10, 9; the lowest is 6, 5, 4, 3, 2.

Four-of-a-kind - four aces is highest, followed by four kings, queens, jacks, etc.

Full house - three cards of one rank plus a pair. The highest-ranking full house is three aces and two kings and the lowest is three 2s and two 3s.

Flush - five cards in the same suit, such as five hearts.

Straight - five consecutive-ranked cards but of different suits such as 4, 5, 6, 7, 8. The highest-ranking straight is A, K, Q, J, 10; the second highest is A, 2, 3, 4, 5 and 6, 5, 4, 3, 2 is the lowest.

Three-of-a-kind - three cards of the same rank such as three aces.

Two pair - two aces and two kings is the highest-ranking combination.

One pair - a pair of aces is the highest pair.

No pair - the best two-card hand in this situation is an ace and king.

There are optimum strategies for forming the high and low hands to increase your chances of winning. Many of these strategies are fairly obvious while others require the learning of specific playing strategies. Here are some tips on how to best set your hand depending on what type of hand you are dealt (i.e., a hand that contains no pairs, one pair, two pairs, flush, etc.).

No Pairs: Play the second- and third-highest-ranked cards as the low hand and the remaining five cards as high hand. For example if you were dealt ace, 10, 5, 9, 3, 2, J, you would set the J, 10 as low hand and ace, 5, 9, 3, 2 as high hand.

One Pair: The pair is set in the high hand and your next two highest-ranked cards as low hand. For example 3, 3, 5, 7, 9, K, 10 you would play 3, 3, 5, 7, 9 as high hand and K, 10 as low hand.

Two Pair: Your playing strategy depends upon the rank of the pairs. If one of your pairs is A, A; K, K; Q, Q, then split the pairs putting the high pair (As, Ks, Qs) in high hand and the other pair as low hand. For all other pairs, play them as two pair in the high hand if you have a king or ace that you can use in your low hand. If you don't have a king or ace, then you're better off to split the pairs with the high pair in high hand and low pair in low hand.

Three Pair: Play your highest-ranking pair in low hand.

Three-of-a-kind: With three aces and kings, split them playing the ace (or king) in low hand and the pair in high hand. All other ranked three-of-a-kind should be played in high hand with your two highest-ranked cards as the low hand.

Straights and Flushes: In general, play the straight or flush as the high hand, the remaining two cards as low hand.

Full House: Play the high pair as low hand and the three-of-a-kind in high hand.

Four-of-a-kind: Always split your four As, Ks, Qs - play one pair as low hand and the other in high hand. With four Js-7s, play them as a four-of-a-kind in high hand only if you have at least a queen that you can use in the low hand. If you don't have the latter, then split the four-of-a-kind (two in low hand, two in high hand). With four

2s-6s never split, always play them in high hand.

Five Aces: Strange as this may seem, you should split the aces and play a pair of aces in low hand, and three aces in high hand.

There are more detailed strategies for other possible card combinations and for those readers who want to learn more, I would recommend the following two books: *How To Play Pai Gow Poker* by Dr. George Allen and *Optimal Strategy for Pai Gow Poker* by Stanford Wong.

Best Bet #10
SINGLE 0 ROULETTE

Best bet #10 can be found on the roulette table.

In general, the majority of casinos offer roulette with 38 numbers on the wheel (so called double zero wheel since the wheel contains a 0 and 00). However, a few casinos offer a single 0 roulette wheel (contains only one zero). The latter reduces the normally high casino advantage of 5.2% for the double zero wheel to a more respectable 2.7%, making it the tenth best bet in a casino.

With a single 0 wheel, any of the standard inside or outside roulette bets have the same casino advantage of 2.7%. So, no matter which bet you make-straight up on a number or a bet on red or black-the casino advantage is the same.

A second option for roulette players to reduce the casino's advantage exists in the Atlantic City casinos because of a rule known as surrender. Here's how surrender works.

If you make outside bets on a double zero

wheel (bet on red/black, odd/even or high/low), and the roulette ball lands on 0 or 00, then only one-half of the wager is lost (or surrendered). This is a mandatory rule for all double zero roulette games in Atlantic City. The net effect is that the casino advantage is lowered to 2.6% for these outside bets ONLY.

Because the Atlantic City surrender option is only available on double zero roulette games and NOT single zero games, you should select the proper game to play depending upon what kind of roulette bets you like to make.

If you enjoy making bets on the inside of the roulette layout, you should confine your play to the single zero roulette wheel since the casino's normal 5.26% advantage on the double zero wheel is cut to 2.70% on the single zero wheel (because of the elimination of one zero). That's a reduction in the casino's advantage of about 2.5%, which is substantial if you consistently play roulette.

If you enjoy making bets on the outside of the layout that pay 1 to 1 (odd/even, high/low, red/black), you should confine your play to the double zero wheel since the house advantage is 2.63% or 0.07% less than the single zero wheel without surrender.

And finally, if you enjoy making both inside and outside bets, then you should confine your play to the single zero wheel. Because even though you give up an additional 0.07% on the 1 to 1 outside bets, you gain much more (2.5%) on the inside bets.

So as you can see, all roulette wheels are not created equal. Be a smart roulette player and learn how to make the tenth best bet in a casino.

Betting Strategies for the
TEN BEST CASINO BETS

Now that you know how to make the ten best casino bets, let's develop a betting strategy that will allow you to maximize profits and minimize losses.

Blackjack

If you intend to play blackjack with perfect basic strategy, I recommend a simple 1, 2, 3, 5 bet progression.

Anytime you win a bet, increase your bet size to the next level. Thus, if you bet 1 unit and win, make your next bet 2 units. Continue to increase your bet size as you win to the maximum 5 unit bet. If you lose a bet at any time, you automatically decrease your bet to the minimum 1 unit. And, of course, you should NEVER increase your bet size following a loss.

In the event you win the 5 unit bet, I recommend locking up the 11 unit profit (1 + 2+ 3 + 5) and starting over again at 1 unit.

If your minimum bet is $5.00, your

progression would be $5, $10, $15, $25. If your hand ties with the dealer, keep the same bet size. If you split a pair and win both hands, or win and tie, you would increase your bet to the next level. Likewise, if you lose both hands, or lose and tie, consider that hand a loss and decrease your bet size to 1 unit.

If betting 5 units is too rich for you, then modify the win progression to 1, 2, 3 back to 1 unit. Or an alternate more conservative win progression is to simply increase the size of your bet by 50% following each win.

The above methods of betting allow you to capitalize on streaks of wins to maximize profits. When you lose several hands in a row, your losses, on the other hand, will be kept to a minimum. And, as a general rule, if you lose 3 or 4 consecutive hands, you should consider leaving the table and playing elsewhere.

An adequate session bankroll would be 20 units with a reserve of at least 80 units. Thus for a $5 basic bet, you should have a session bankroll of $100 and a reserve bankroll of at least $400.

If you are card counting, then size your bet depending upon the count (as explained earlier). An adequate bankroll for a card counter is fifty times the maximum bet. Thus, if 4 units is your maximum bet, you should have a 200 unit bankroll. (A $20 maximum bet, requires a $1000 bankroll for safety).

Craps
For the pass line and come bets, use the

following 50% betting progression:

    $3, $5, $7, $10, $15, $25, $35, $50, $75, etc.

Every time you win, increase your bet to the next level. When you lose a bet, revert back to your minimum bet.

It is not necessary to start at $3. Your minimum bet could be $5, $10 or $50 and your 50% progression begins from this bet size.

Naturally, you should always make the proper odds bet with each bet on the pass line or come.

Your session bankroll depends upon how many bets you intend to make. If all you will be betting is pass line with odds, then your session bankroll should be 10 times the amount of the minimum pass line, plus odds wagers. If your minimum bet is $5 plus $5 odds, this yields a total of $10. Your session bankroll should be $100 or ten times $10.

The same betting strategy can be used for the don't pass and don't come bets.

Roulette, Baccarat, Pai Gow Poker

You can use the simple 1, 2, 3, 5 win progression or the 50% win progression for the bank/player hand bets in baccarat, the 1 to 1 payoff outside bets in roulette (odd/even, high/low, red/black), and for pai gow poker.

I normally don't encourage casino players to use any kind of betting progression that increases the bet size following a loss. The one slight exception is the following unique progression called Oscar's Grind[4] which keeps the bet size at the same level following a loss. This betting system is conservative with a goal of winning only one unit on each series of bets. It's easy to master and will allow you to enjoy many winning sessions where you can win a relatively small amount of money. The kicker is that like any other progression, a long series of losses could wipe you out. But we'll set stop losses to prevent this from happening.

Assuming a starting bet of 1 unit, the rules of OSCAR'S GRIND are as follows:

1. Increase the size of the bet by one unit following a win.

2. Maintain the same size bet following a loss.

3. Never bet more than necessary to recover past losses suffered during a series plus a one unit profit.

Quit a session when:

---

[4]This betting method first appeared in Alan Wilson's book, *The Casino Gambler's Guide* and then later modified by Tom Anisile (*How to Gamble in a Casino*) and by Bruce McClarren (*Gambling Times Magazine*, June 1983).

4. You've won one half the size of your playing session bankroll or

5. The losses are down by more than 10 units and your next bet would place you down 20 units or more.

The key to the betting scheme is rule 3, ie only bet enough to win 1 unit to end a series.

Let's try a series of wins and losses to explain the betting method.

Example

bet (units)	1		1	1	1	2	2	2	3	1		1	1	1	2
decision	W		L	L	W	L	L	W	W	W		L	L	W	W
net	+1		-1	-2	-1	-3	-5	-3	0	+1		-1	-2	-1	+1

The first bet in series #1 is 1 unit. You win the bet (decision W). Your net is +1 unit. Since you're ahead 1 unit and this is the goal of OSCAR'S GRIND, pocket the 1 unit and start another series. This series begins with a loss. You're down 1 unit. Because you lost the 1 unit bet, you again bet 1 unit (rule 2). This bet also loses. You again bet 1 unit (rule 2) and win. This leaves you down 1 unit for the second series. Since you won the 1 unit bet, you increase the bet to 2 units. Unfortunately, this bet loses. The next bet you make is also 2 units (rule 2). This also loses, putting you down 5 units for the series. The next bet is also 2 units and wins. You are now down only 3 units. The next bet size can be increased to 3 units since the previous 2 unit bet won (rule 1). You win the 3 unit bet leaving you even. Even though you won the bet, you only make the size of the next bet 1 unit according to rule 3 (you only want to bet enough to end a series with a 1 unit profit). Luckily, the bet wins and you are ahead the 1 unit which you pocket.

Practice the OSCAR'S GRIND betting scheme on paper and convince yourself you can win small amounts. But remember rule 5 - don't put yourself into too deep a hole - stop increasing your bets if you are down by 10 units and a loss would put you down 20 units or more. This rule will prevent you from getting totally wiped out - don't forget it!.

MONEY MANAGEMENT

Until now, I've been discussing playing and betting strategies. But knowing this isn't enough to be successful in the casino. You must also learn how to manage your money.

Consider this scenario. The gambler learns a good playing strategy, perhaps one he read in a good gaming book, and after many hours of reading and practicing the playing strategies at home, he heads for Atlantic City armed with his knowledge. He knows his playing strategy will give the casino only a very tiny advantage, so with a little bit of luck he should win.

Our gambler begins to play and proceeds to win a small amount. Then, suddenly, things start to go wrong and he starts to lose his winnings. Before long he finds himself still losing and his pile of chips is diminishing. In the midst of this losing streak, our gambler begins to double up on his bets. "After all," he figures, "the fastest way to get even is to increase my bets. The dice (or cards or wheel) have been lousy and I've got the feeling that my luck will turn." So after making maybe $5 or $10 bets up to now, he begins to wager $20, $25 even $30 at a clip. After all, with a couple of big wins he'll be even.

Most of you probably know the ending to this story. Before long our gambler loses his chips and reaches in his pocket for more money. He pulls out another couple of $100 bills and thinks, "this will get it all back for me!" Where it maybe took 1 hour to lose the original bankroll, now it takes only 15 or so minutes to lose another $100. But the dice or cards or wheel have to turn, so again he goes digging in his pocket for more cash. Before long our gambler is tapped out, another victim of poor money management.

How can you avoid this scene? First of all, you must learn to hang on to your profits in casino play. This is, after all, one of the advantages you have over the house; namely, you can quit playing anytime you want to. But when the average gambler is ahead, no matter what, it's never enough and greed sets in.

To be successful in the casino you must discipline yourself to quit a winner. A small profit, after all, is better than no profit or a loss. Be content to leave with a 50% profit based on your session bankroll. For example, if you start a session of play with $200, plan to walk if you can manage a $100 profit. That's sensible and smart play.

More important than disciplining yourself to quit with a profit, is disciplining yourself to cut your losses. This simply means you should first of all never commit more than 20% to 25% of your

total bankroll to any one session. If your total
bankroll is $500, bring only $100 to the tables and
quit the session if you lose $100. This will give
you a chance to rest and think about what
happened (were you playing accurately or were
you confused and making costly mistakes)? And
you still have $400 left to try your luck and skills
at another session.

Finally, you should never try to play "catch-
up" by increasing the size of your bets. No matter
how skillful you are, you will be experiencing
sessions where nothing you do seems to go right.
Like doubling down on the blackjack tables with
your 11, drawing a 9 and watching in disbelief as
the dealer pulls a five card 21. Or playing your
favorite roulette number all night in a losing
cause, only to switch numbers and then have your
favorite number win. This is part of gambling that
every player must come to expect. But you must
prepare yourself for these inevitable occurrences.
Never increase your bets in the hopes of trying to
get even. And always quit a session if 20% to 25%
of the bankroll is lost. If you learn to confine your
losses to small ones, the profits will more than
compensate for your losses.

Let's rewrite the story of the unfortunate
gambler that I told you about at the beginning of
this chapter. He has a $1000 bankroll and he
comes to the tables to play with $200. He plays
blackjack with perfect basic strategy and is
somewhat of a counter. He begins to lose but he
keeps his cool and doesn't press his bets (unless
the count would indicate a large bet). Soon he

begins to win and finds himself $150 ahead. He plays a few more hands, loses them, then he pushes back his chair and leaves with a profit.

If you learn to manage your money like this, as well as learn how to play properly, you will join an elite group of casino players who, in the long run, will win more money than they lose.

PSYCHOLOGY OF GAMBLING

Learning proper playing strategies and sound money management principles is only part of a successful casino gambler's game plan. Having a proper playing attitude is just as important.

The typical attitude of losing gamblers is something like this: They always go to the casinos to have fun and of course, they always expect to lose. They experience an emotional high when playing and are invariably swept up in the exciting casino atmosphere. They always feel obligated to take the free drinks offered by the casino as a way of getting even for their losses. And, of course, when they lose, they always blame it on rotten luck, or poor cards, but the consolation for their losing is "well, I had a good time anyway," attitude.

Now, don't get me wrong, having fun should be your first objective when you gamble. But that doesn't mean you shouldn't try to win.

Keep this thought in mind next time you go to a casino to have some fun. First, when you enter a casino, you are entering a place of business. And like all successful businesses, the casinos are operated by shrewd businessmen whose job is firstly, to keep you playing and happy and secondly, to separate you from your money as quickly and painlessly as possible. To meet these objectives, they create an atmosphere in the casino that can be described as a "Disneyland for adults." No clocks to let you know it's time to leave this utopia, no windows to let you see out to the real world, free drinks at the tables, free lounge shows and plenty of pretty girls to keep you happy and playing.

And what happens to the average gambler when he enters this casino designed excitement? For him, the rewards of winning all of the casino's money far outweigh the risks of losing his meager hundred dollar bankroll. And this exciting atmosphere also makes it so easy for the average player to feel lucky and go for broke at the chance of winning that jackpot.

First and foremost, in order to be a winner, you must learn to control your emotions in the casino. As Lyle Stuart, casino gaming author, puts it: "The real struggle when you are playing is, in most cases, not between you and the casino, but between you and yourself." You will find plenty of temptations to keep you playing and losing, therefore, you must learn to develop a sense of timing or awareness of when to play and, more importantly, when to quit.

In short, you must develop the proper playing attitudes to overcome the psychological barriers created by the casinos to keep you losing and to make it difficult for you to leave the tables with a profit. For example, go to the casinos expecting to win (rather than lose). Granted, there are no guarantees that you will win, but likewise there is no guarantee that you have to lose. Always prepare yourself for those inevitable losing sessions. No matter how skillfully you play, sometimes everything will go wrong. Will you quit and call it a day or will you be like most gamblers and dig in for more cash, hoping the tide will turn? And how many gamblers have the attitude that a small profit is better than no profit or a loss? Not many.

Above all, learn to develop a sense of timing for when to play and when to quit. Playing blackjack, for example, if you are tired or have been drinking will cost your dearly.

These attitudes are not always natural. Most of them take an amount of work before you can feel comfortable playing with discipline. But if you develop these proper playing attitudes and learn proper playing and money management strategies, you will be able to enjoy the fun and excitement of casino gambling with a minimum risk to your bankroll. Isn't it worth the effort?

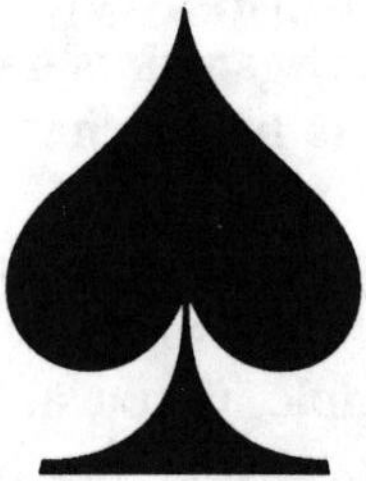

SUMMARY

The ten best casino bets are:

Blackjack
Craps - pass line/come with odds
Craps - don't pass/don't come with odds
Baccarat - bank hand
Baccarat - player hand
Craps - place bet 6/8
Video Poker
Craps - lay bet 4/10
Pai gow poker
Roulette - single 0 wheel

To be a winner in a casino, you must make only the above bets using a proper betting scheme and money management. Go to the casinos with a proper attitude that you are there to have a good time but you intend to give the casinos a fair fight for their money using all the playing and betting skills available to you. Your biggest advantage is the fact that you can quit playing anytime you want. Therefore, try to discipline yourself to quit a session a winner. Winning a small amount is a lot better than losing or breaking even. Just remember that you can't be a winner until you learn to quit a winner. Good luck and play smart.

Recommended Reading

The following books are recommended to further increase your expertise about the casino games.

Fundamentals of Blackjack, by Carlson Chambliss and Thomas Raginski

Professional Blackjack by Stanford Wong

The Dice Doctor by Sam Grafstein

Winning Casino Craps by Edwin Silberstang

All About Roulette by John Gollehan

Winning Baccarat Strategies by Henry Tamburin

Optimal Strategy for Pai Gow Poker by Stanford Wong

Expert Video Poker by Lenny Frome

Henry Tamburin on Casino Gambling by Henry Tamburin

Index

Baccarat, 31
Bank hand, 33
Bank hand third card strategy, 34
Banker, pai gow poker, 53
Basic strategy, blackjack, 6
Betting strategies, 63
Blackjack, 3

Caller, 33
Card counting, blackjack, 13
Casino advantage, 1
Co-banking, 54
Come, 22
Come-out roll, 19
Commission, bank hand, 35
Commission, lay bet, 46
Commission, pai gow poker, 53
Computer simulation, 4
Craps, 19

Dependent trial process, 4
Don't come, 29
Don't pass, 25
Double odds, 21

High hand, 49

Insurance, 11

Lay bet, 45
Low hand, 49

Mini-baccarat, 36
Money management, 69
Multiple action blackjack, 12

Natural hand, baccarat, 33

Odds bet, 20
Oscar's Grind, 66

Pai gow poker, 49
Pai gow poker hand rankings, 55
Pai gow poker playing strategy, 56
Pass line, 19
Place bet, 37
Player hand, 33
Player hand third card rules, 34
Playing attitudes, 74
Playing rules, blackjack, 16
Psychology of gambling, 73

Roulette, 59
Running count, 14

Single odds, 21
Single O roulette, 59
Surrender, blackjack, 9
Surrender, roulette, 60

Tie bet, 32
Triple odds, 22
Video poker, 41
Video poker playing strategy, 43

Win progression, 64

PUBLICATIONS BY
HENRY TAMBURIN

Blackjack: Take The Money and Run. Win at blackjack! This book will teach you how to walk away from the tables with profits. Contains the basics of how to play plus beginners, intermediate, and advanced level playing strategies. $15.00.

Blackjack - Deal Me In Video. This 90 minute, professionally produced video was filmed in a Mississippi casino and features Henry Tamburin demonstrating the basics of how to play blackjack with tips on how to improve your chances of winning. $34.95.

Craps: Take The Money and Run. Learn to play craps like a pro! Contains the basics of how to play, plus winning techniques including the unique Increased Odds betting system. $15.00.

Craps - Rolling To Win. This 90 minute, professionally produced video was filmed in a Mississippi casino and features Henry Tamburin demonstrating the basics of how to play craps with tips on how to improve your chances of winning. $34.95.

Reference Guide To Casino Gambling (2nd ed.). Concisely explains the playing rules and optimum playing strategies for 25 popular casino games. $15.00

Winning Baccarat Strategies. The first book to present effective card counting strategies for baccarat. $20.00.

Pocket Blackjack Strategy Card. A durable, plastic coated, hand held card that contains the complete basic playing strategy for blackjack. Take it with you to the tables and always make the correct play. $3.00.

To order any of the above, send check or money order payable to Research Services Unlimited, PO Box 19727, Greensboro, NC 27419. (Above prices include shipping and handling.)